Flower Arranging For Complete Beginners

Eleanor K. White

Introduction

This is a comprehensive resource for individuals interested in learning the art of creating beautiful and captivating floral designs. The guide covers a wide range of topics related to floral arrangements, from the basics of design concepts to step-by-step tutorials for creating various types of arrangements.

The guide starts by exploring the reasons behind people's love for flowers and introduces the concept of pursuing a floral career. It then introduces the five fundamental steps of floral design, explaining why the author finds the 5-step approach valuable. The steps include container preparation, cleaning and processing of flowers, categorizing flowers into line, feature, and filler categories, adding final foliage and decorative elements, and finishing touches.

Tools commonly used in floral design are discussed in detail, including floral foam, containers, floral tape, wires, gauges, greening pins, knives, mosses, and more. The guide provides insights into the usage of these tools and how they contribute to creating well-structured and visually appealing floral arrangements.

The guide also covers the basics of color theory, texture, and the color wheel as they relate to floral design. It explains different color combinations, such as monochromatic, analogous, complementary, split complementary, triadic, tetradic, and paired complementary schemes. The importance of color selection and coordination in creating harmonious floral arrangements is emphasized.

Flower identification is another essential aspect covered in the guide, with detailed information about various types of flowers like Hypericum, Queen Anne's Lace, and Spray Roses.

The guide includes a series of tutorials that walk beginners through the process of creating different types of floral arrangements. These tutorials cover various techniques such as preparing floral foam, wiring flower heads, making boutonnieres, crafting corsages, creating hand-tied bouquets, arranging roses in vases, making topiaries, designing fan-shaped arrangements, crafting small basket arrangements, and much more.

Throughout the tutorials, readers are provided with step-by-step instructions, accompanied by images, diagrams, and explanations to help them understand the techniques and concepts behind each arrangement.

In summary, this book is a comprehensive resource that provides beginners with the knowledge and skills needed to create stunning floral designs. From understanding the basics of design principles to hands-on tutorials for crafting various arrangements, this guide serves as a valuable reference for anyone interested in exploring the world of floral design.

Contents

CHAPTER 1: *About You, Why You Like Flowers*

"There are always flowers for those who want to see them." - Henri Matisse

Why do you like flowers? Do you want to become a professional floral designer? Maybe an event planner? Are you thinking of some other vocation which allows you to work with flowers and natural materials? Do you want to help a friend out with their wedding, or maybe even do your own wedding flowers? Even if you don't want to do any of these things, the common uses for flowers in everyday life are reason enough to take your floral design skills to the next level.

You have probably had events in your life which were improved by the presence of flowers. Flowers improve almost any situation. At one of the shops I worked in, we had a dance instructor who came in and bought flowers for each child in the recital. I wrapped the little bouquets with extra ribbons hanging down so the child would feel like a princess (or prince). Even if you're only trying to sell your house, floral design can come in handy. Real estate companies agree that homes with fresh flowers show much better. The reasons to become more familiar with floral design are myriad when you take a moment to think about all the special occasions there are in one year alone!

Just having a basic knowledge about floral design can help you create something for any of the following occasions:

1. Birthdays - Bouquets, table arrangements, decorations

2. Baby showers

3. Valentine's Day

4. Halloween - You may think that Halloween is a "dead" (ha) time in the floral business, but you can make an adorable pumpkin arrangement and beautiful cornucopia arrangements.

5. Thanksgiving – Centerpieces, topiaries, or a beautiful fall bouquet can make a big difference at this celebration.

6. Holidays such as Christmas, Chanukah, and Ramadan. Almost every religion or faith honors the presence of flowers.

7. Get Well wishes for an under-the-weather friend, co-worker, or family member. A few flowers arranged in a coffee mug for a friend who is ill can make a bright spot in their day.

I'll bet you can think of many more! We seldom think of using flowers as often as we could for enhancement of all the occasions I mentioned above. If you read my book and follow the basic instructions for the five steps, you should feel confident enough to create something great for any occasion.

Far from frivolous, becoming better at floral design can be a cost-effective and useful ability. Learning how to arrange flowers attractively for any occasion will instantly put the power into your hands! I suggest you "freestyle" a few bouquets from the local store.

Treat yourself to a bouquet or two of mixed flowers, a block of floral foam, and a container. Take your materials and flowers and practice creating different kinds of arrangements with what you have in your bouquets. When you're done with your first one, remove the flowers and re-use them in a few different arrangements. You will get to know the stems better this way, and you are likely to have a wonderful time while the flowers tell you more about themselves!

Try separating your flowers and foliage into groups and considering the different kinds of things you can make with only a few colors, or only one color. Experiment with corsages and wiring and taping the flowers if you can. Invest in a few basic tools and supplies and then invest in yourself by buying a "play bouquet" every now and then that you can open and use to create your own designs. Don't be too hard on yourself if you are disappointed with what you make. Remember that you probably won't stop loving flowers, so why not keep trying? If you need to see pictures of floral designs to copy, try visiting the online wire services such as Teleflora and FTD. Have a look at the arrangements they are selling and get a good look at the flowers they're using, the container styles, etc. I love the international wire services and what they have to offer. Familiarize yourself with their products, styles, and services.

I want to mention that if you are giving the arrangement you are making as a gift or want it to last, don't re-use floral foam or flowers.

A florist would not re-use floral foam because it can become moldy and shorten the life of your flowers. Also, the foam can lose its integrity and flower stems might not be able to drink. However, if you don't have a huge budget for floral foam, I suppose you can re-use it one extra time if you need to for your learning purposes.

A Floral Career

As mentioned above, it is important to put in the time necessary to learn the flowers and their stems to learn floral design best. However, you can learn a fair bit of information through online tutorials, books, and the like just by observing.

Maybe you want a floral career and you've purchased this book as a step along the way in your floral education. A floral career can be wonderful, but unfortunately it doesn't come with a high salary. Many floral designers make little more than minimum wage, except for the top designers working for extremely high-volume shops and ateliers. However, the landscape of a flower shop owner is much more hopeful than that of a worker.

If you can open a shop of your own and run it in a cost-effective way in a good location, your opportunities to rake in the profits multiply greatly! By "cost-effective," I mean being careful with your assets including fresh floral materials and the number of assistants you hire.

Within the retail floral world, much of the time it's quiet except for bouquet customers and your basic orders which might come through the Mercury system (like Teleflora and FTD). During this time, you don't need many assistants because business doesn't support the extra labor. However, you will need them when the busy times such as Valentine's Day, Mother's Day, and Christmas arrive. This can be a challenge as you don't want to make anyone feel bad about occasional part-time work. This is the reality that a floral shop owner must deal with. Still, if you are considering opening your own floral business, it's probably a good way to go. If you just want to work as a florist, it may be harder to make money. That said, it's a great way to learn!

By "good location," I mean you must research what areas are not currently served well enough by any flower shop. I'm sure you can easily see the value in this. If you open a shop in a mall, make sure that you're not spending too much on rent. If you can find a good building that you can buy or rent reasonably, that's the best situation for having a successful (money making) flower shop.

Whether or not you want to be a pro, I hope you find this book helpful for your needs.

CHAPTER 2: *The Five Steps*

Why I Feel 5 Step Floral Design is a Worthwhile Concept

It took me years to make sense out of the enormous variety of flowers, foliage, and materials used in floral design. After years of learning what is and is not used most often, it occurred to me that I had never really seen or heard of any floral design books or information which tried to "break it down" for the floral design student. Separating flowers into mental categories with respect to how they will be used in your arrangement can eliminate a lot of confusion, and you can get started more quickly and work more confidently.

When you think about it, most floral design work, large or small, consists of five basic elements.

These elements do not always occur in the same order, and they sometimes occur in stages, however, they can be divided into five distinct categories.

THE FIVE STEPS

1. Preparing Container, Wires, Foam, Framework, etc.
2. Line Flowers, Structural/Architectural Elements
3. Feature Flower/Mass Flower
4. Filler Flower
5. Foliage/Greening, Finishing, Ribbon, Card, etc.

Most arrangements from corsages, to bouquets, to wedding and funeral arrangements contain these five elements in some way. Of course, there are exceptions. Sometimes you will use only one kind of flower, or one color, etc. For now, let's not concern ourselves with exceptions, but only the basic ideas I'm putting forth in this publication because I don't want to confuse you.

If you are just starting out in floral design, it can be hard to even know which flowers you are working with, let alone which flowers are considered most advantageous to use for each step. It takes a while to learn which flowers are considered Architectural/ Line, Feature/Mass, or Filler Flowers.

Some have multiple uses depending on the overall arrangement, but this also takes time to learn. By breaking it down for you so that you know right away which flowers are considered which, you can more easily and quickly navigate the landscape of the designs you intend to create. My intention is to introduce you to many of the most used flowers and then show you how to create some commonly and uncommonly used arrangements using my 5 STEP FLORAL DESIGN technique.

I will be showing you many of the techniques and supplies used, such as floral foam, tapes, and wires in Step 1, then on to the flowers used in Steps 2, 3, and 4. Step 5 (Foliage and Finishing) consists of learning about foliage and what a good ratio of types and colors to choose for your arrangement is. This step, as with all the steps, can take place in a different order. If you want to place greenery first, that's fine, however, it is still a distinct step to be followed, no matter the order. This "finishing" step may also be where you add a bow, some special wrap, etc.

The Steps

I want to stress that the five steps are more of a mental concept, rather than step-by-step directions which must be followed in order. You can use them in order if you like, but if you don't want to, you will still benefit from knowing them. Steps 2, 3, and 4 are concerned with categorizing flowers used for different parts of the design. This is the bulk of 5 Step Floral Design - which flowers to choose for which part of the arrangement and why. For instance, let's say you want to create a centerpiece for an upcoming dinner. Right away, let's plan for this:

Step 1- Container. Let's use a festive, gold-painted basket. Prepare it with floral foam and tape.

Step 2- Structural/Line flowers. I would like to buy six white snapdragon flowers for the structural elements.

Step 3- Mass/Feature flowers. Next, let's spend on some beautiful red roses to catch the eye. I think we will need nine of them.

Step 4- Filler Flowers. Now we might choose to fill in with baby's breath (gypsophila).

Step 5- Greening/Finishing. Fill in with your chosen foliage. At this point, look at it and see if there is anything else you want to add. If not, make sure you've covered up your mechanics with enough greens, add any ribbons and additional elements like wrapping or a card, and you're done!

That is the basic idea of 5 Step Floral Design.

Adding More

Within every stage, you may choose to use more than one flower from that step's category. You may also choose to use no flowers from a step's category. You may choose to use one type of flower from Step 2, two types of flowers from Step 3, and one type of flower from Step 4.

I hope it's not confusing, but the point is that as long as you remember which flowers you are using for which step and why, you are free to do anything you want. Hopefully you will see that knowing which flowers you will use for each part of your arrangement ahead of time helps you to be more mentally organized and stay within your budget.

Much of the time, which flowers you use will be relative to the other flowers you're using. Flowers are chosen for their variances in size, shape, height, and color. They are also chosen for budget and placement. Ultimately, it's up to you.

Step 1 - Preparing the container or foam, tapes, etc.

In Step 1, I will discuss some basic methods to choose and prepare your container. We will also go over wires, tapes, floral foam, and securing everything down so that we will have a nice, sturdy starting point. This is so important. The flower tape does a serious job of holding everything together, so we need to spend time making sure it's secure!

Cleaning and Processing

When flowers first come in from your supplier they will need to be processed. This process can take hours and is usually given to a junior member of the team. Many hate it, but I always loved it. Each flower requires a different process.

Flowers come in bunches and boxes from all over the world and locally. When they arrive you have to process each stem separately. Roses, for instance, require a few processes. To give you an idea of the process for just one kind of flower – roses – the steps are as follows:

1. Remove the rose from the roll. Remove the lower third of the leaves from the rose's stem.

2. Use rose stripper to remove all thorns or remove them manually with a knife.

3. Take off the top two or three petals. These are called "guard petals." You can keep them if you like but don't store them in the fridge with the other flowers as the gasses released as the floral material decays can affect the living flowers and sometimes make them die more quickly.

4. Give the stem a fresh cut, diagonally. 99% of the time a diagonal cut of the last inch or so of the stem is made right before putting the rose into a solution. This might be the second solution for the roses, as roses often receive a special treatment in addition to the basic treatment.

There is a similar process to what I've described above for every flower and piece of foliage that enters the shop. This can be time-consuming and is usually done by a floral assistant. Personally, I find it relaxing. I go on automatic mode when I'm cleaning flowers, especially if the radio is on and there's a coffee nearby! Cleaning flowers is a necessity in a real flower shop, but you won't usually learn how to do it in flower school.

Step 2 - Line Flowers or Structural Flowers

These flowers vary depending on the type of arrangement you are doing. Generally, they have a strong, tall, or otherwise commanding element and we place them first. These flowers are used as a structure upon which the rest of the design can be built around. Usually, they are some of the more expensive flowers within the arrangement, but not always. We will go over the flowers most often used for this purpose.

Step 3 - Feature or Mass Flowers

Feature flowers and mass flowers are showy and usually more expensive. We place these according to how we placed our first flowers.

Step 4 - Filler Flowers

This usually means the more plentiful, but less showy flowers such as baby's breath, limonium, waxflower, etc. Sometimes flowers from Steps 1 or 2 can be used when they are taken off the stems and used individually.

Step 5 - Greening or Adding Final Foliage, Cards, Accent Items such as Gold Bullion, a Bow, or Anything Else Needed to Finish Off

Greening is one of the steps which can be done at any time. Some find it easier to start with containers greened, and some find it easier to place the flowers first, leaving most of the greening for last. Still, some like to work with it as they go. Whichever you choose, it's an important step. I'll talk about techniques for greening and types of foliage commonly used. We will also go over how to create a Florist's Bow. This puts the power of fantastic bow-making literally at your fingertips! If you have to buy them, it's not uncommon to pay ten dollars for one bow, but once you get the hang of it, it's one of the easiest things to make and I will show you how!

The above steps are worth going over again because this is the bulk of what 5 Step Floral Design has to offer. If you can organize the steps and the flowers ahead of time, you can quantum leap your floral design ability. Even if you are a seasoned florist, if you need to explain techniques to your students, or anyone, 5 Step Floral Design offers a new way to help your students understand floral design concepts more quickly.

"When you have only two pennies left in the world,buy a loaf of bread with one, and a lily with the other." ~Chinese Proverb

CHAPTER 3: *Tools Used In Floral Design*

A lot of the magic of floral design is a result of tools and techniques. Below I've included some of the tools floral designers often use.

Floral Foam/Oasis

One of the first things I thought was magical about floral design is floral foam, which is sometimes called by one of the big supplier brand names, Oasis. Since in this book we're only talking about fresh flowers and not silk or dried ones, we will only be using wet floral foam, that is, foam for fresh flowers.

Long ago, before floral foam was widely used, floral designers had to use floral tape and wires to create many arrangements. One of the interesting lessons I learned from my flower school days was how to create a bouquet of old. This consisted of wiring and taping every blossom and element used in the bridal bouquet. No one does it this way anymore, since floral foam revolutionized the industry.

Floral foam has come into question in recent years because it can contain some chemicals meant to extend the life of flowers. This might be objectionable to you if you avoid chemicals. Some innovative companies are developing new floral foam alternatives. Currently floral foam is the most used solution for arrangements. For most of the arrangements that you will create, except for vase arrangements or flowers to wear, you will be using floral foam. As easy as it is to use, it still requires technique to take full advantage of it.

How to Use Floral Foam

Before you begin your design, cut off a piece of floral foam or use the whole brick and drop the foam into a container of water with floral food (please see recipe below for homemade floral food if you don't have any from the store). Allow about 20 minutes for the foam to soak up the water, slowly sinking deeper into it unassisted. You don't want to push it down or force it because this can create air bubbles in the foam which I'm sure you can guess is not good for the flowers. If the stems are placed into foam and don't reach water but instead reach air pockets they will not be able to do their job of delivering water to the flower heads.

Another thing to keep in mind about floral foam is that it is unbeatable for large-scale design work. It can be stackable and easy to use if you secure it well to your container with strong, thick floral tape. In wedding work, floral foam can be broken up and taped to arbors or put into pew holders to hold small, tasteful accent flowers for a wedding venue. It's hard to imagine modern day floral design without floral foam. I'm still in awe of it!

Below is a display of floral foam and Styrofoam in many of its forms. However, you can create almost anything from the humble block foam style.

Above, the bridal bouquet of this lovely, vintage bride shows how bouquets were made with wires and tape before the advent of floral foam.

Earlier I discussed floral foam for wet flowers. There are other kinds of floral foam and materials which look exactly like wet floral foam but are very different.

Floral Foam for Silk Flowers

This one is easy to spot because it's the harder block of floral foam and is very sturdy. This is specially made to support the stems of silk and artificial flowers. Of course, when I say "stems" in this case what I really mean is plastic and wires. The foam is strong, but if you are doing silk floral design work, you will most likely need to use glue, such as in a hot glue gun. Of course, using hot glue materials for fresh flowers is discouraged as they should be kept away from heat sources, but it's perfect for silk flower arrangements.

Floral Foam for Dried Flowers

This foam is often overlooked because not too many people realize the difference between it and the dry foam for silk flowers. I've done a bit of design work with dried flowers and can tell you that the stems (which are real, not plastic or wires) will not take the hard foam that's made for silk flowers. The stems of dried materials are often delicate. The floral foam for dried flowers is a softer consistency and it's easier to glide the brittle stems down into the foam. So, if you decide to try your hand at dried flower design work, look for the foam that's made for dried flowers. Some of them say "for silks and dried flowers," but don't be fooled. If you're doing dried design work, it's worth it to look for the special foam.

Your Container

In Step 1, we consider our container. This can be a vase, a plastic designer's bowl, an elegant urn style container, or a whimsical coffee mug. For funeral arrangements, you may use a mache pot, which is an urn created with a paper/cardboard substance. Much of the time, mache pots are used to keep the value of the arrangements concentrated in the flowers. Containers never stop evolving for floral designers and I find it exciting! That said, there are still a few tried and true container options which customers seem to choose again and again.

The most used containers in floral design are baskets, vases, and plastic florist's designer bowls. These are quite versatile; you can fill almost any floral order with one of these three container options. Another benefit of these options is that they are usually color-neutral. You may be surprised to find that choosing a container that does not fit into the general theme or is not in a complementary color to the flowers can really skew everything. Choosing the right container affects the whole arrangement.

Other Forms

There are many forms created for assisting the floral designer. You can purchase large ones in the shapes of hearts and wreaths for special work such as funeral work. These are great, but you don't need them to create large floral designs. It's worth it to check out the various forms available in supplier's catalogs and craft stores.

Floral Tape

Floral tape is one of the two basic kinds of tape we use most often in floral design. You use it just like regular tape, where the adhesive is only on one side. It also has some waterproof qualities (it's sometimes called waterproof tape), although you must be careful not to get it wet before you stick it to your container. Floral tape comes in many colors but in a flower shop, I usually use three kinds:

1. The thinner kind for small and delicate work. Usually in a dark green color.

2. The thicker kind for almost any larger work, or even smaller work if you like. Usually in a dark green color as well.

3. The transparent kind. This is the one I reach for most often as it looks great with any kind of clear container such as a vase.

Floral Tape is used in many aspects of floral design, most importantly to secure your floral foam down into your container. Usually, you only need a few pieces, but sometimes you need a lot and when you do, you're glad it's there! It's quite miraculous for holding it all together.

Flora Tape

Not at all like regular tape, flora tape is another staple of floral design. It is also known as stem wrap, and that is its main use - to wrap stems.

How to Use Flora Tape

Flora tape takes some time to get used to handling correctly. The tape has no adhesive quality until you stretch it slightly. This releases the glues and makes the tape adhere to itself. You want to wrap your stem tightly while pulling the flora tape tightly around it as you go. You don't want to pull the tape out to release the glue beforehand, as this will make the flora tape lose its sticky qualities. It must be done as you go, using a pull and twist motion. I realize it's hard to explain, but if you buy a roll of it, you will see! Be careful though, because craft stores can incorrectly label it floral tape, but professional suppliers will list it as flora tape.

Floral Wires

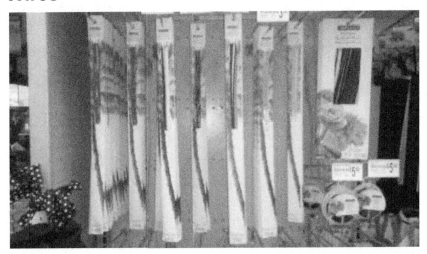

I know that wires seem like the furthest thing from floral design, but they are one of the most important tools for professional floral arranging.

Gauges

There are heavier and lighter gauges of wire for your use in floral design. They all have their places, but most of the time I only need to use a few specific gauges. Some of your work will require a heavier gauge, such as a 22, but most of your work will likely rely on a softer gauge like my favorite, gauge 26.

Much of the time, the wire you use will depend on a specific flower you are wrapping. Sometimes a 26 gauge is not strong enough, so in this case, I reach for stronger wire. However, if you want to get started, go ahead and start with gauge 26 wires.

Wires for floral use usually come as straight, single pieces. I find that paddle wire is also helpful as it's easy to unroll and use as needed. You will find that you usually need to cut your wires to size.

Greening Pins

(Shown in tutorials)

A cute little item used to help secure materials to the container is the greening pin. They remind me of hairpins, except for flowers, ha! They're handy for placing ribbons, mosses, greenery, and anything else you need them for. Once you use them it's easy to see why florists do.

Wreath Wrap

This is a roll of plastic wrap, usually green. It is most often used to help secure floral foam to wire forms. It is often used in funeral work and the creation of memorial headstone pieces and wrapped around wreath frames filled with wet sphagnum moss as an alternative to larger floral foam forms.

Various Dried Mosses

I love it when I can incorporate moss into my arrangements. In a flower shop, you can order it and it usually comes in boxes. It is still green and fresh when purchased this way. You can also purchase various types of dried mosses from floral supply stores and craft shops. Some mosses can use a bit of rehydration with a few sprays of water, but dried moss does not need to be rehydrated and many do not rehydrate.

Sheet Moss - Usually green and comes in flattish sheets.

Spanish Moss - Dried and great for hiding last minute open areas in some arrangements.

Sphagnum Moss - Can be rehydrated and is beautiful for the same uses as Spanish Moss.

Bun Moss - Similar in appearance to sheet moss, but in the shape of a small mound. Since it's more solid than many other kinds of moss, it can be used more structurally.

Deer Moss - A spongey-looking moss, it gives character to design work where needed. It comes in many colors and is great for contemporary looking arrangements.

Knives

A small, sharp knife works best. In floral design work, knives are the industry standard. This intimidated me at first, but I eventually learned how to use knives in my floral design. I don't want to brag, but I became so good at it that I was considered super fast by my co-workers. I have never cut myself working with knives in floral arranging, however, I did cut myself once with pruners!

If you are intimidated by using knives, I can't honestly say that I think you need them for floral design. You can do everything with pruners (not scissors) that you can do with a knife. You don't have to use knives if it's not comfortable for you. The reason knives are considered the best way to work with floral material is two-fold. One, the cut you make in your stems is likely to be sharper and cleaner which keeps bacteria out and maximizes the stem's ability to take in water. Second, like using good form to reduce keystrokes on a keyboard, using knives is generally faster and you know how important that can be in a flower shop! You may not need to be fast, though. You are most likely not planning a floral career, but simply want to learn how to use flowers in the best ways. In this case, there is no need to be the fastest florist on the block, so it's okay to use pruners.

More Items

Pruners - Pruners are useful for cutting hard stems and branches, finishing off the stems of bouquets, and much more. Again, if you're not using a knife, it's okay to use pruners for cutting your stems but don't use scissors, as they are not strong enough to cut most stems. You will need pruners either way!

Excelsior - A creator's helper, excelsior has the look of raffia or moss but is made of shaved wood. Having it on hand can be useful when you least expect it for final touches.

Wire Picks

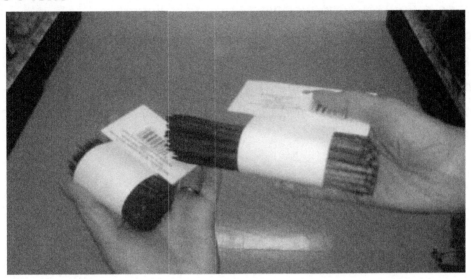

These come in a few sizes. A wooden pick with a wire wound on one end may not sound like it would be useful in floral design, but this handy little item is great for adding last minute touches to your arrangement. They are often used to attach things like pine cones, fruits, or other elements to your work.

Corsage Bracelet - These have really evolved as of late. We used to have a simple cardboard and wire elastic thing to attach our corsage work to. Nowadays, we have many different options such as rhinestone and pearl looking bracelets upon which you can top your corsage work. The other kind still exists and is widely used.

Lomey Dish/Items - Lomey is a brand name of helpful items used in floral design. They are structurally helpful plastic items which can sometimes be put together to make larger or more commanding arrangements, usually for weddings and special displays. They are mostly used in flower shops and only available from professional suppliers.

Colortool - Floral spray paint.

Crowning Glory - A spray-on floral hydrator and extender. Often used as a final touch in wedding and funeral work.

Pokon/Leaf Shine - A spray-on luster-inducing cover that imparts a glossy look to foliage.

Floral Preservative - It's good to use the kind from the florist that comes in packets, but if you don't have any, you can mix up a batch at home.

Ingredients:

  1 quart water, not too cold or too hot

  1 teaspoon bleach

  1 teaspoon sugar

  2 teaspoons lemon juice

Why do the flowers need floral preservative? Floral preservatives usually contain three important things for the flower's longevity. The bleach keeps the stems from collecting bacteria, the citrus adjusts the PH levels, and the sugar feeds the stem. This is not the same as flower food you would give to a living plant or flower; it contains bleach which can kill a living plant.

CHAPTER 4: *Color Basics, Texture, The Color Wheel, and Some Commonly Used Floral Design Terms*

Other Terms in Floral Design

Scale

Scale refers to the sizes and values of all the elements of your arrangement in relation to each other.

Proportion

The relation of a section of your arrangement to the rest of it.

Balance

Using colors in such a way that all the elements including the dark, light, warm, and cool colors are placed appealingly. Colors that are warm carry more weight (visually), while lighter colors seem less heavy.

Rhythm

When we speak of rhythm in floral design, we mean using something - usually color - to unify the whole. This is often achieved in floral design by creating repeating patterns in your design, which help to carry the eye throughout.

Texture

Along with choosing our floral shapes, texture plays an important role. It is a good idea to examine the textures of your chosen flowers and foliage for their differing qualities. Using three different kinds of foliage can add more than just green to your design work.

Shape

While creativity is king, and any flowers put together in a vase or arrangement are worthy of appreciation, if we pay close attention to the different shapes we choose, we can create more visually interesting arrangements. As a beginner, sticking with a few flowers is a good idea to keep it simple. Let's say you're going to use three kinds of flowers for your arrangement and it's going to be to based on roses. Other than that, you have tulips, daisies, and snapdragons available to you. Of those flowers, I would not choose tulips because their shape is similar to that of the rose. I would choose to add daisies and snapdragons because their shapes are quite varied from that of the rose. Having said that, tulips and roses can be quite lovely together, but it depends on the arrangement and the overall look you want to achieve. In general, try to vary the shapes of the flowers you use to add contrast and interest.

Focal Point

The focal point of an arrangement is where the eye is directed within it. It is usually somewhere around the middle, but not always.

Hogarth

William Hogarth was the most famous English artist of his time (1697-1794). He wrote a book called *The Analysis of Beauty*. In the book, he asserted that the curved "S-shape" in all it's subtle and pronounced forms contributes greatly to pleasing design.

Above, plate 1 from William Hogarth's Book Analysis of Beauty.

The World of Color in Floral Design

Hue, also known as color, is a complicated subject. My hope is to start you off without complicated theories of the why and how of color usage. My aim is to give you a few simple principles and ideas to work from. When you get a chance to learn more about color, it will greatly enhance your floral design experience.

A Few Basics About Color

The three primary colors (red, yellow, and blue) have the power to produce any other colors you wish. Added in equal parts you can get orange, green, or violet. When you combine equal amounts of primary and secondary colors, you get what is called a tertiary, or intermediate color.

Hue = Color

Value = How light or dark that color is

Chroma = The intensity or saturation of a color (hue)

Tint - You produce a tint when you add white to a hue, making it lighter and giving it the ability to reflect more light.

Tone - You produce a tone when you add gray, neutralizing the hue.

Shade - You produce a shade when you add black to a hue, making it darker in value, reflecting less light.

Warm, Cool, and Dependent

Warm Colors

Reds, oranges, and yellows are warm colors. These seem larger and can give the illusion of moving toward you. It's good to remember that a warm color will seem more dominant in your arrangement.

Cool Colors

Blues and violets are cool colors. Unlike warm colors, which seem larger, cool colors seem further away.

Dependent

Green is not cool or warm. It does not advance or recede. However, when changing its tint, tone, or shade by say, adding extra blue or yellow, a piece of floral foliage can have warm or cool qualities.

The Color Wheel

The color wheel can be a big help with your floral design work. Once you understand basic color theory you will find it much easier to whip up amazing designs which are pleasing to the eye for more than one reason. However, it also can be confusing. In this book, I break down how to quickly choose colors and how many to choose.

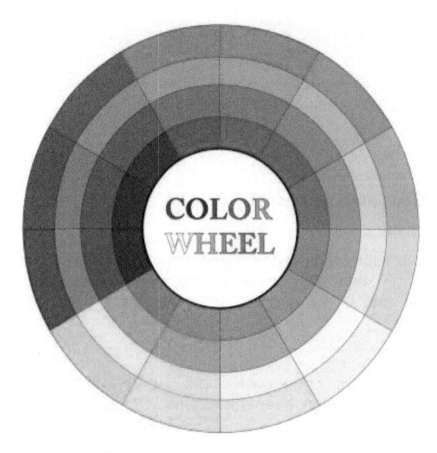

Types of Color Combinations

Monochromatic Color Scheme

This usually means using only one hue with its tints, tones, or shades. White, black, and mid-grey are considered achromatic because they have no hue.

Analogous Color Scheme

Using one primary color with hues, tints, tones, or shades on the color wheel forming a 90-degree angle.

Complementary (Direct)

Colors which are directly opposite on the color wheel are considered complementary (orange and blue, violet and yellow, green and red). You can't go wrong if you use complementary color schemes.

Split Complementary

This uses three hues. This time, we choose our main hue, but instead of using the hue's direct complementary, we choose the two colors right beside the hue's direct complementary. For instance, if I choose yellow as my main hue, using red-violet and blue-violet instead of violet would be considered split complementary.

Triadic

Using three colors equally distant on the color wheel makes a triadic color scheme.

Tetradic

Using four colors equally distant on the color wheel makes a tetradic color scheme.

Paired Complementary

This is usually considered more advanced and happens when you use two pairs (at least four total) of complementary hues.

A Few Words About Color in Floral Design

Unlike a painter who can create any color he or she likes, florists must use what nature has created. You can't take three primary flowers and make different flowers, ha! You may not always have the colors on hand to create the perfect color scheme.

I have found that sticking to just three types of flowers and three colors in your arrangement will help the overall design. You will usually have a few white flowers on hand. White is considered neutral on the color wheel. Using it with two other colors can create a pleasant effect.

Colortool Floral Spray Paint

Colortool is a spray paint specifically for flowers. It is not like regular spray paint; using regular paint on flowers is not recommended. This kind of paint is lightweight and comes in many colors. It's meant to be used on delicate petals without causing them to wilt or die.

One of the biggest helpers in the floral industry is a can of light blue Colortool. Why is this, you ask? While some of nature's flowers have blue, the flowers we use in floral design do not include many truly blue flowers. The closest you will find is some hydrangea, blue/purple delphinium, dyed blue dendrobium orchids, or some grape hyacinth. These are somewhat blue-purple tinged. Whatever shall we do for the baby boy arrangements? Enter light blue Colortool!

If you have any white flowers on hand, you can spray them with the Colortool for instant baby boy joy! I've also used color tool in some of my large design work. I have used silver and white paints on exotic foliage such as bird of paradise and pineapples, giving them the look of cold metal and machinery. You can also use it to touch up any colors in your arrangement that don't look as nice or match as well as you would like.

There are so many possibilities with Colortool. If you get a chance to play with it, you may enjoy it as much as I do! At the very least, if you open your own flower shop, don't forget that one can of light blue!

CHAPTER 5: *Flower Identification Guide*

Here I've included some of the most used flowers in professional floral design. It by no means attempts to cover the entire world of flowers that are available to you locally or worldwide. As a professional floral designer, I learned that there are a few flowers which are available year-round by many suppliers for a reasonable standard market rate. These flowers are often called for by most of the international wire services such as FTD and Teleflora. These amazing international services have helped standardize many of the floral designs and flowers which you as the florist are expected to have on hand to fill orders. I've found that many flower shops have a combination of these standard flowers on hand at all times, but also any number of interesting and local flowers available to them as well. There can be great variety based on your location and it is a lot of fun to work (and play) with unusual flowers.

In this book, I only want to familiarize you with some of the most often used flowers that you find in the flower arrangements in those pretty pictures on the websites of the wire services. The reason this is useful to you is because florists worldwide use the wire service books to help clients define and relate to the florist the kind of arrangement they want. When you go into a flower shop to order flowers, you don't have to describe in your head what you want, you usually see it in one of the wire service's design books at the flower shop or online. Much of what you find in those books are arrangements which use many of the standardized, available-year-round flowers. As I've said, this is only a partial list, and I'm sorry I have to leave out any flowers at all, but I hope this at least gets you started. Enjoy!

Alstroemeria

An extremely useful and long-lasting flower, it is usually used for our Step 3 (feature/mass) or Step 4 (filler flower) placements. It comes in many color combinations and is one of the staples floral designers can't do without.

Anthurium

Anthurium is an extremely commanding tropical style flower. We would use it most of the time as a Step 2 (line/structural) or Step 3 (feature/mass) flower, but never for Step 4 (filler).

Asiatic Lily

Asiatic lilies do not usually have any fragrance and are used in Step 2 (line/structural) or Step 3 (mass/filler) placements.

Bird of Paradise

Bird of Paradise is considered a tropical style flower. Step 2 (line/structural) placements are usually most appropriate as not too many other flowers are more commanding!

Carnation

Carnations can be used for Step 2 (line/structural), Step 3 (feature/mass), or Step 4 (filler), depending on your other flowers and the overall design of your arrangement.

Gerbera Daisy

A gorgeous flower with no fragrance, it usually needs to be supported by a gerbera tube or a wire inserted using the "hook" method. It's usually used as a Step 2 (structural/line) or Step 3 (feature/mass) flower.

Gladiolus

Gladiolus comes in many colors. It's long-lasting and normally only used as a Step 2 (line/structural) flower. The top few unopened pods are usually snapped off by your local florist to control the line of the flower, but that's a matter of taste. Often used in funeral and wedding arrangements, they are a florist's staple.

Gypsophila (Baby's Breath)

Gypsophila normally comes in a few different sizes. There is a larger variety and a smaller variety called Million Star which has gained popularity. While some flower shops do not use it, I find it to be beautiful and elegant when balanced well within the context of your other design work. In the picture above it's gorgeous all by itself, but usually it's used as a Step 4 (filler) flower.

Hypericum

Such things as berries and rosehips can add visual "items of interest" within your arrangements and bouquets. Alas, many berries and rosehip bundles do not come on long stems. Enter hypericum. It's sturdy, long-lasting, and has strong, long stems allowing it to be used in bouquets as well as any other type of arrangement which calls for something like berries. It's usually used as a Step 4 (filler) flower but can be used as a Step 3 (feature/mass) flower as well.

Liatris

A strong, long-lasting, and visually unique flower, liatris is usually a Step 3 (feature) flower or a Step 2 (line/structural) flower. I say them in that order because although liatris is tall, it's not wide enough to command much of a structural presence. For this reason, it's likely to be used in a supporting role such as a Step 3 (feature) flower.

Limonium/Caspia

A beautiful alternative to gypsophila, limonium comes in white, pink, lavender, and other colors. It's long-lasting and usually reserved for Step 3 (filler flower).

Mini Carnations

Like larger carnations, mini carnations are extremely useful to the florist. Fragrant and long-lasting, they can fill the role of Step 3 (feature/mass) or Step 4 (filler).

Asters

Usually available in white, pink, and lavender, asters can be used either by individual stems or as a whole in a bouquet. They usually fill the role of Step 4 (filler) but are sometimes used as Step 3 (feature/mass) flowers.

Mums (Daisy)

Daisy mums, and other kinds of mums, like flat mums, which come many blooms to a stem, are another one of the florist's besties. In a flower shop, you always want to have them on hand at least in white, pink, and yellow. Cost-effective and with no fragrance, they can be used as one stem of many blooms in a bouquet, or the stems can be used individually. That's one of their greatest uses in floral design. The daisy mum is not very expensive, but it is one of the few flowers which can work well in Steps 2, 3, or 4.

Mums (Chrysanthemum)

These are normally used as Step 2 (structural/line) or Step 3 (filler/mass) flowers. They're too large to be a Step 4 (filler) flower.

Oriental Lily

These usually have larger blooms than the Asiatic lily and are highly fragrant. They're normally used for Step 2 (line/structural) or Step 3 (feature/mass). I'm sure you can see why they're not used as a Step 4 (filler) flower.

This is a good time to tell you about pollens. Have another look at that beautiful lily. Lurking right before your eyes can be one of the florist's worst nightmares - pollen! Because pollen can easily transfer to the flower petals, your hands, and just about anything else including a bride's dress (yipes!), it's great to reach in there with a bit of tissue and remove the pollens completely. If you do it early enough the pollens won't be mature yet and won't transfer their color.

Queen Anne's Lace

This is a stunning and unique flower which is most often used as a Step 3 (feature/mass) flower or as a Step 4 (filler) flower. It is an extremely tall and stately flower with strong, large heads. A vase full of them is commanding. They are not usually considered a Step 2 (structural/line) flower, but they can be if you are so inclined. In some areas of the world they grow wild and can be thought of as weeds, but in many other areas they are non-existent.

Rose (single stems)

    Single-stemmed roses come in many different stem lengths and for the most part, their cost is directly related to the stem length. In general, a florist should have long-stemmed roses on hand for any bouquet or vase arrangement orders, but they should buy some of the shorter-stemmed roses from their supplier as well. These can be used in many of the arrangements for which the longer-stemmed roses are not necessary because you will cut the roses shorter to put them into an arrangement anyway. Roses are usually reserved for Step 2 (line/structural) or Step 3 (feature/mass).

The Meanings of Roses

Red	I Love You and/or Beauty
White	Purity and Spiritual Love
Yellow	Happiness and Joy
Coral	Desire
Orange	Enthusiasm and Fascination
Lavender	Love at First Sight
Pink (light)	Admiration
Pink (dark)	Gratitude, Thanks

Snapdragon

Tall, frilly, and feminine looking, snapdragons come in a variety of lovely colors. They are usually considered Step 2 (line/ structural) flowers but can sometimes be used as Step 3 (feature/ mass) flowers.

Solidago

Another amazing flower, solidago can be used as a Step 2 (structural/line) flower or a Step 3 (feature/mass) flower. It's mainly used as a Step 4 (filler) flower. As you can see, it has individual stems upon the main stem which are useful to break off and use as individual rays of yellow throughout your arrangement. It is strong and long-lasting.

Spray Roses

Spray roses are another one of those great little helpers for florists. Mainly used as Step 3 (feature/mass) and Step 4 (filler) flowers, they come many to a stem and can be used as a whole or individually.

Statice

Very long-lasting, statice is normally used as a Step 4 (filler) flower.

Waxflower

A tiny flower with a delicious, subtle fragrance, waxflower is one of my favorites. It's usually used as a step 4 (filler) flower.

Cymbidium Orchids

One of the more expensive orchids, cymbidium orchids are quite long-lasting. They are popular in a lot of contemporary looking designs and are mainly used as Step 2 (line/structural) flowers, but also as Step 3 (feature/mass) flowers.

Dendrobium Orchids

Sturdy and coming many to a stem is the dendrobium orchid. Unlike the cymbidium orchid, this is not one of the more expensive flowers, yet it is versatile and long-lasting. It is normally used as a Step 2 (structural/line) flower or a Step 3 (feature/mass) flower.

Oncidium Orchid (Dancing Lady)

A stem with many tiny flowers, each flower resembles a small dancing lady in a beautiful flowing dress. The oncidium orchid is usually used as a Step 4 (filler) flower.

Phalaenopsis Orchid

One of the more reasonably priced orchids, phaelenopsis can be used as Step 2 (line/structural) or Step 3 (feature/mass) flowers.

CHAPTER 6: *Tutorials*

PART 1 - Preparation & Finishing
How to Prepare Floral Foam
Soaking Floral Foam and Using Floral Tape

1. Have a container of water deep enough to cover the floral foam entirely. If possible it's good to have already fortified the water with flower food/extender mix. (Please see recipe here for flower food or use the kind from the flower shop

that comes in packets). Drop the floral foam into the water source and allow it to slowly submerge on its own.

2. Allow the floral foam to soak for at least two minutes or more if possible. Don't ever try to force the foam down into the water because this will create air pockets, which will make it harder for stems to access water and nutrients.

3. After waiting for the foam to soak, I've placed one whole block of the foam into my container. In this case it's a long

plastic florist's design container. You can place your foam however suits your needs. If you only need a smaller piece, it's best to cut it off before you soak it.

Here, I've taped my whole foam block into a design container and then wrapped it around the whole foam and the container. I've used thin but strong floral tape and wrapped it around the foam and container both horizontally and vertically, a few times around. If I were to hold it upside down I am sure that everything would stay in place.

This is not the way you have to do it all the time. In fact, you would usually just tape the container over the edges as you can see in some of the taping of the arrangements in this book. I do however want to impress upon you that structural integrity is very important in floral design. When using foam for an arrangement everything should remain in place if you shake it around a little. As a rule of thumb, use as few materials (such as tape) as possible because they eat away at your budget, but use as much as you need to be sure your arrangement will stay put.

How to Wire a Flower Head

Wiring and Taping Using the Cross Method

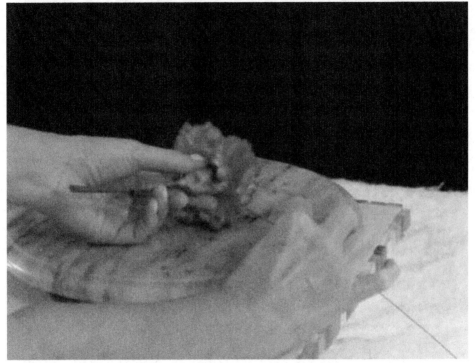

1. This method is used for large head flowers such as heavy rose heads. I first insert my wire directly into the bottom area of the flower across and through the calyx.

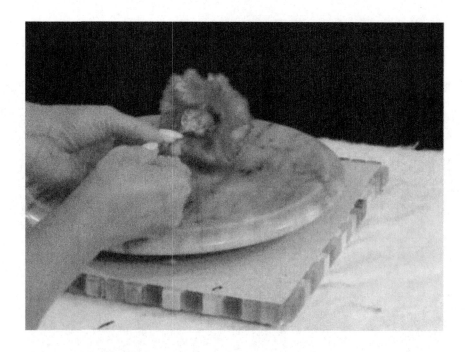

2. I then take the wire and bend it back up to criss-cross once
    again through the calyx, but this time on the other side.

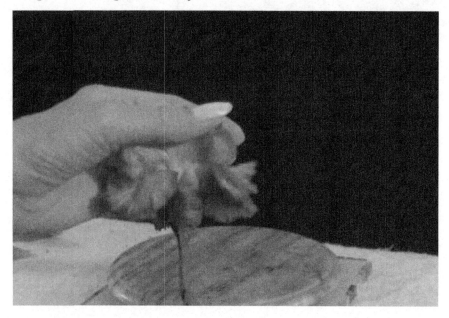

3. I've smoothed all the wires down and covered them with flora tape (stem wrap).

How to Make a Boutonniere

Create a Boutonniere Using the Soft Method of Taping and Wiring

1. For this tutorial, I'm using single blooms from alstroemeria flowers. Unlike the other methods shown in this book, we will use the soft method. Basically, any time a flower has a head which seems too small or delicate to insert a wire through, you tape it with flora tape first, then insert the wire.

2. Here I have taped my alstroemeria.

3. Next, I've inserted my wire through the middle and then bent it down to resemble a stem.

4. I've wired and taped two alstroemeria and chosen some bear's grass to create more visual interest.

5. I've taped my bear's grass in the middle after bending it into a loop. Additionally, I've chosen some other elements for my boutonniere.

6. Hold the pieces together and arrange them in your hand until you like the way they look. Place your flowers (two in this case but you can use more) in front of the base items and move them around (touching the wires mainly) until you like the placements. Tape the whole thing together with flora tape.

7. You can choose to wrap the entire stem but since we did that in other tutorials in this book I thought that a more natural stem look might be a nice change.

8. Here is our finished alstroemeria boutonniere, alongside our daisy corsage also from this book. As you can see it is possible to get very creative with corsage and boutonniere work! Sometimes it can be hard to keep them from looking too busy, but you can add bows, beads, and pretty much anything you want!

For corsages, try to use white tipped pins or pins to match the arrangement, while boutonnieres (meant for men) are generally given black tipped pins. Boutonnieres and corsages are typically worn on the left side.

Boutonnieres and corsages can be as rustic or as diamond studded as you like!

How to Make a Daisy Corsage

Create a Daisy Corsage Using the Hook Wiring Method

1. This method is appropriate for any kind of flower head with a daisy type of flower. Start underneath the flower head.

2. Insert a medium gauge wire up through the bottom of the
   flower head, right through the top. Once the wire is
   extended through and past the flower head, bend it into a U
   shape and pull it back down through the flower head again.
   This is almost invisible to the eye! Then wrap the wire
   around the stem and tape as usual.

3. Some leaves and groups of leaves do not need to be wired. However, it's a good idea to wire any leaves you are unsure of. Simply insert a bent wire about one sixth of the way down the leaf, as shown. Then twist the wire down to form a stem and cover it with flora tape, as with other stems shown.

4. Assemble all your elements and decide whether you need wire and tape. In the case above, I've wired my daisies and my leaf, but the stem of the solidago is already pretty strong so I'm not going to wire and tape it.

5. I've decided to add one more piece of greens here with my leather fern. I've placed everything together as I like it and then wrapped everything over once again with flora tape. I could have cut this one shorter, but I like the look of a long stem, so I made a little curly cue by winding the wrapped stem around a pen.

6. For any corsage or boutonniere, don't forget to add pins so that they can be pinned onto the recipient. As I've mentioned elsewhere in this book, it's fine to use regular pins, but it always adds a special touch if you can give your clients something better, such as pins which match the flowers. Those small touches can really make a difference.

This is a wrist corsage. You can create a wrist corsage the same way as a pin-on style corsage, but you need something to hold it to the wearer's wrist. There are many great, new corsage base bracelets with rhinestones and artificial pearls which give the wearer a keepsake to enjoy after the event is over. There is also a cardboard style available.

How to Wire a Pinecone

A Technique for Wiring Pinecones and Other Items

1. Choose a pinecone that is the appropriate size and shape for your overall arrangement. Use a heavy gauge wire if possible, 26 or lower. The lower the gauge, the stronger the wire. Place the wire on the lower third of the pinecone.

2. Wrap the wire around the pinecone and twist a few times to make it secure. Pull the wires down to give them the look of a stem. Tape with flora tape if you need a finished look, otherwise use it however you need, hiding the wire if possible.

How to Make a Florist's Bow
Crafting a Hand-Tied Ribbon Bow

1. Take a length of ribbon. If you want to make one small or medium sized bow, it takes about one yard or more. This is for a six-loop bow. You can use less expensive ribbon for this, or more expensive ribbon, the choice is yours! Some ribbon is wired like the one in my tutorial. I personally love wired ribbon, but some people find it cumbersome to work with.

Step one is to take your ribbon by one end leaving a tail of about eight inches, then make a small loop and twist it. This will be the center of your ribbon.

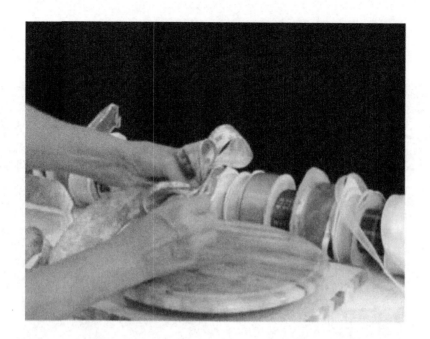

2. While holding everything firmly, create a second loop and twist it. Create six alternating loops like that, each time twisting the loop and holding the whole thing firmly in your hands.

3. Once you've got your loops together and they seem relatively even, move on to the next step.

4. Notice the criss-cross twists under the ribbon.

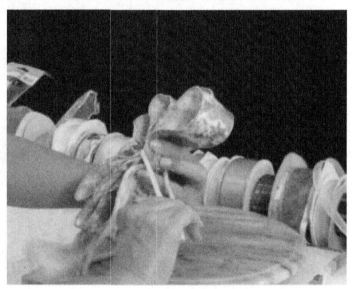

5. Take a chenille stem (yes, it's a pipe cleaner, but don't let a florist hear you call it that, ha!). Try to use one which matches your ribbon. Place it over the top of your bow, to one side of the middle loop (the first small loop you made which is actually loop seven). Secure the chenille stem by twisting it enough times that your bow is nice and firm.

6. I'm finishing off my bow by making sure my tails are nice, clean, and even, and not straggly. You can cut your ribbon sideways or in a dovetail. Fluff up your ribbon's loops and form them to make a beautiful bow.

This method can be used to make small or large bows. However, sometimes when you need to make large bows it's best to create a few smaller ones and then put them together to create a larger one. If you are fresh out of chenille stems, you can use pre-taped floral wire, but it does not grab and hold onto the fabrics quite as well as the chenille stems.

TUTORIALS PART 2
Floral Arrangements
How to Arrange a Dozen Roses with Gypsophila in a Vase

1. My vase has been washed well and is ready for me to create a vase design.

2. Using five large, shapely leaves, create a flower grid by inserting them one by one until they look like a star.

3. Now choose five more nice, firm leaves and place them over the first grid of five, one by one. This time you will alternate the placement of leaves to be opposite the leaves already placed.

4. I added a few tall salal branch stems toward the top and middle areas. I've also added my gypsophila. In this case, it will be too hard to add it in later, after my roses have been placed.

Notice the large mouth of my vase. This is something to consider when making vase arrangements as the larger the mouth of the vase, the more floral material must be put in to support the roses. This is of course up to you and your budget.

5. I started by establishing where my number one rose would be placed - straight in the middle and slightly higher than most of the other floral material. After that I placed my next six roses evenly around the lower outer areas, then placed the next five in a zig-zag pattern equally distant, in the middle area, all around.

6. I've added variegated pittosporum and a few other touches, and we're done!

Designer arranged vases are one of the things you spend a lot of time creating in a flower shop. Deciding what kind and size of container you will be working with ahead of time will help you plan how much floral material you will need to use.

Shifting into mini-mode, this small vase still needs enough floral and foliage material to support the structural flowers. Pre-planning your stems in relation to your vase is a big part of creating any successful vase arrangement.

In the small vase arrangement I created above, even though I used three large-stemmed carnations, I still had to add other elements to support the flowers. Sometimes this is done with foliage, as in the case above where I used solidago and bear's grass.

How to Make a Hand-Tied Bouquet
Hand-Tied Bouquet Using Six Carnations

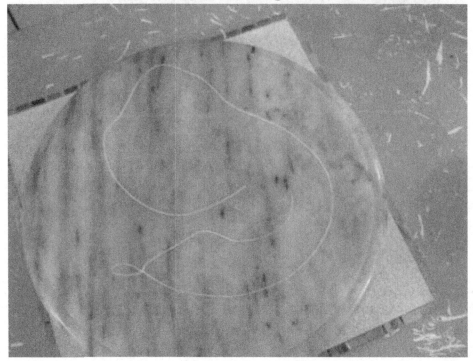

1. I've taken about two feet of florist's wax thread and tied it into a loop with about six inches left at that end and set it aside.

2. Next, I've chosen three kinds of foliage, one taller foliage stem, and three each of salal and leather fern. Using a loose grip on the greens, I hold them so that I can now add individual flowers into the middle and throughout the bouquet.

3. I added two stems of gypsophila early on, so I will have no problems with it later. You may have to work it around a bit so that it's evenly placed.

4. Add the first flower in the middle, followed with three more surrounding it but slightly lower down.

5. Add in the last two flowers and work with them in your hands to get them as even as possible.

6. I've decided to add some variegated pittosporum mostly toward the bottom areas. The next step is to take your piece of wax thread and whip it over the top of your bouquet stems, wrapping the wax thread around and around a few times until it is firm. Put the end of the wax thread back through the loop and tie it to the other end. Tie the bouquet so that it's firm but not squeezing any of the stems too tight. Hold the finished bouquet up in front of your intended vase and use your pruners to make a nice, clean cut, just before inserting into your vase.

Note: You can see through my vase where my wax thread has been wound around the bouquet. It's usually good to try to cover up such things. In a case like this, try adding some feathery greens like plumosa fern to extend around the collar of the arrangement and hide your wax mechanics. A nice bow works well too.

How to Make a Tall Topiary

1. For this arrangement, we are using one full block of wet foam and two more small pieces recessed inside the container, but lower down. The small blocks will help to anchor the whole in place and I've made sure everything is very firm. For instance, that block of foam in the middle is solid because I've placed the other two pieces of foam right next to it to keep it firm. Also, this container is watertight, but yours may not be. It's always good to put some plastic or a container inside if you're not sure of the water tightness of the vessel you're using.

We have placed our floral tape criss-cross in the middle, but this time we've made it slightly off center because the topiary "tree" form of alstroemeria will need to be inserted a few inches in, close to the center. If the tape is in the way it can be harder to do this.

2. I've taken my closely bundled six stems of pink and white alstroemeria. While holding the top part of the stems and the bottom area, I've inserted all stems at the same time. Sometimes I will wrap the stems with ribbon or tape before this stage to secure the bundle as a unit, but in this case, I've inserted them all at once, about three inches down into the container.

Tip: As I only had alstroemeria of a certain height, but wanted them to appear taller, I set the foam up higher, coming further out of the container, lending more height to the alstroemeria.

3. This is actually part of Step 5 (greening and finishing). However, this is one of those times we can use a step out of order. I want to insert twigs, but it may be harder to insert them if I wait until all the other flowers are placed. Also, you can ruin an arrangement that way.

When using branches and twigs, sometimes you have to work with them to get the effect you want. In the example above, I've inserted the twigs both into the lower foam and the higher foam. This is to be sure it's all anchored well, but also because I want the twigs to curve naturally and so I had to make concessions with the natural shape of their branches, then lasso them in and tie them at the top.

4. I've inserted my most important flowers for this arrangement (the alstroemeria). These are the ones which will be seen the most and in this case are the most expensive. This is often the case, though not always.

Next, I've inserted white flat mums in a radial fashion around the center of the topiary. Notice that they are only in the top foam. I've also created an arbor looking effect by tying the two twigs together with wire at the top. Today I'm using cherry tree branches, but you may find curly willow more available year-round.

5. The picture above shows Step 4, which is the filler flower (in this case it's baby's breath). I've also dotted it around the areas below where I've placed my white flat mums.

6. In this case, Step 5 consisted of adding three kinds of greens (salal, variegated pittosporum, and leather-leaf fern) to hang down slightly over the edges in a few places. As I wanted to pull the pink shade of the alstroemeria through the whole arrangement, I've added a light pink ribbon by winding it through areas of the arrangement and tying it at the top. After that, I attached a separate ribbon to the top to secure all the ribbons firmly and make it look like the whole thing is one ribbon. I've also taken some of the sections of the ribbon and secured them with greening pins to give that loose and airy feel, all the while keeping the arrangement firm.

How to Make a Fan-Shaped Arrangement
12 Roses in a Fan Shape

1. Here you can see that we have already placed our soaked foam and taped it well to the container as this will be a heavy arrangement and placed our first leaf at the top to help establish height. We have also placed our two side leaves equally distant on both sides. We are beginning the formation of our fan shape.

I want to mention that I used one entire block of floral foam and placed it sideways. I could have put it in flat, but I wanted to have a lot of the floral material extending upward, so I chose to place it sideways.

2. Using the leaves that are already placed as guides, here we have inserted our fourth and fifth leaves. We're trying to keep a basic fan shape with our first leaf placements.

3. Here we've placed our first flower. In this case it's a rose and it's used as a line flower even though it's not traditionally considered a line flower. Any straight and tall flower can be used as a structural base the same way a line flower would (like a snapdragon or gladiolus).

Place this rose slightly above your first leaf and insert it into the back third or so of the foam. You'll want to leave plenty of room for the rest of the flowers and foliage!

4. Now we've placed our second and third flowers, establishing the width of the arrangement, again trying to keep them in the back third of the foam.

Although I did not rest them on the container's edges, you can do that if you like. It's good to do so because you establish the bottom area of your structure and leave fewer mechanics that will need to be covered up in the long run.

5. Now we've added flowers four, five, six, seven, and eight. At this stage, look for a diamond shape from your middle flower up to your top flower. These flowers have been added in the foam in the middle areas.

6. Now we're placing roses nine, ten, eleven, and twelve. These flowers will be placed in the upper third, forward, top part of the foam and in the front area of the foam.

7. I'm starting to fill in my open areas now with my feature flowers or mass flowers, in this case white flat mums, using mostly larger flowers on the lower areas and keeping the upper flowers smaller. I've had to strategically cut my mum stems to provide enough blooms for the effect I'm going for.

8. In this picture, I've added in more white flat mums on the outer areas of the arrangement. Notice that I have not extended these flowers outside of where the rose borders have been established. This is one of the ways to keep your arrangement tidy along the way.

9. This picture shows Step 5 (greening and finishing), but I wanted you to see that I'm starting to begin Step 5 at this earlier stage. Here I've used salal.

10. At his point, I was not sure if I wanted to just use greens (variegated pittosporum) or gypsophila, so I first added in the variegated pittosporum, then added in pieces of gypsophila after that. Next, I finished off the greening in the back.

I thought about using a bow in this arrangement but decided against it. Much of the time adding a bow to an arrangement can be like "gilding the lily." Even though I love bows and using non-floral materials in the realm of floral design, it can become gaudy when too much is added.

There is a great quote by Marilyn Monroe. I'm paraphrasing here, but she said that whenever you are going out and you have your outfit on, turn away from a mirror and then turn back to it quickly. If you notice anything that catches your eye first, like a piece of jewelry, remove it. I think that's a similar idea to adding bows and beads to floral arrangements. In some cases it's wonderful, but in other cases it may be more appropriate to stick to a natural feel. The choice is yours, and that's one of the wonderful things about floral design; there's plenty of room for creativity!

How to Make a Small Basket Arrangement

1. We've taken roughly half of a brick of soaked floral foam and secured it to the sides of the basket. This is a special basket which came from a floral supplier, with its own plastic insert to help with waterproofing. If you do floral design work in baskets, be sure to add some other water barrier inside, such as plastic wrap or a container.

2. These tall, commanding phlox will be my first structural flowers.

3. I placed it near the middle of the foam and to one side of the basket handle.

4. Our second phlox flower is placed slightly lower and as part of a triangle.

5. Our third flower completes the triangle, but as you can see the three phlox flowers make up a staggered triangle, with different heights on all sides.

6. Now I'm placing my large mums lower, in a way that they can be seen from both sides of the basket. I would normally use three of these mums, but one shattered while I was working with it. Some kinds of mums can easily shatter and be ruined. For this reason, I'm going to make up the difference with other flowers of a similar visual weight and place them where a third mum might have been. It's often necessary to improvise at the last minute.

7. Now I'm beginning my outer framework by placing mini carnations in strategic areas to form an outer skeleton.

8. Continuing to turn my arrangement as I work, I'm now filling in all those areas with other plant materials. I've added in pieces of variegated pittosporum and individual spires of solidago.

9. I've added in mauve daisy mums, some recessed back in the arrangement and others on the outer areas. My final touch was to add limonium and a few mini carnation buds.

How to Make a Long, Low Hogarth Centerpiece

1. Starting with my soaked foam and taped container, I insert a leaf on the side to begin to establish length.

2. I've created a greened container for a centerpiece using ten leaves. Often in a flower shop you will pre-green such

centerpieces to later be filled with flowers for orders.

3. This centerpiece will have Hogarth elements to it. I'm beginning by placing my first three roses coming out of the corner area of one of the ends of foam, starting with the longer one and then zig-zagging inward.

4. Your fourth rose will establish the height. Place the fourth rose in the middle of the top and higher than the other roses. To place the roses on the other side, use the first

three roses you placed as guides. Match them to the opposite side, also coming out of the corner of the foam. This is called "mirroring technique."

5. Here I've started to add in some mums. I've placed them evenly in a zig-zag pattern, with larger flowers toward the middle and smaller ones reaching out from the ends. You can see here that the roses are placed coming out of the corner area of the foam.

6. Here is a front view of the addition of white mums. Notice the mums are placed further down in the arrangement than the roses. This adds depth.

I want to point out that because this arrangement has Hogarth elements, I'm trying not to add anything distracting along the edges or sides that may take away from the gentle Hogarth S-curve. This Hogarth curve will start low and rise in the middle, then drop at the other end again.

7. I've added in some green mums, variegated pittosporum, and gypsophila.

8. I added some long Israeli ruscus stems on each end and accented with bear's grass to help define the Hogarth shape.

The centerpiece pictured above is also a long, low centerpiece, but does not display a Hogarth element.

In a flower shop you are asked to create centerpieces of all kinds, but in my experience, none are so popular as the style pictured above, which is another version of the long, low Hogarth centerpiece in this tutorial.

How to Make a Tall, Pedestal Hogarth Arrangement

1. I'm using a tall glass container into which I've placed moss. Next I will insert a small block of floral foam which extends a few inches out of the top of the container, so that I can have some of the flowers cascading downward. I'm using clear floral tape for this arrangement.

2. Starting in the middle with my first carnation, then placing the outer two carnations next, makes it easy to see where the last two carnations need to go.

3. After placing the carnations, I placed my white mums and mini carnations and zig-zagged them from one end to the other. I then placed my large, white mums close to the middle to reinforce my focal point. Finally, I formed several stems of bear's grass together and put them at the top and bottom of my Hogarth form, so that the shape is intensified. Though I prefer to place it directly on the table, here I placed it on top of a container for better visibility.

How to Make a Small Triangle Arrangement

1. Here we begin with a gold-tone container which is already prepped with our soaked foam and tape. My container is terra-cotta painted gold, which will go nicely with the soft pinks I plan to use for this arrangement.

2. First establish your height with your first leaf, then your width with leaves two and three. In general, you want your second and third leaves to touch the container at the base of the foam.

3. I did a little more greening than I usually do at this early stage. I want to show you how pretty foliage is on its own. If you are a beginning florist you can gain confidence by doing more of your greening first, as it's easier to see your form and shape emerging before you insert the flowers.

4. I'm using two pink carnations as the center of this arrangement. I've placed the top one in the middle and the second one is slightly staggered to the right.

5. Now I've chosen one long, strong flower from a stem of many mums. To the right, you can see that I've trimmed off all the other flowers except for the one I need to sit at the top. The other flowers will also be used, but lower in the arrangement.

6. I've placed my one long daisy mum at the top of the arrangement and this will form the top of my loose triangle.

7. Taking some of those shorter mums from the stem, I've put one directly in the middle in front and one on each side,

completing our triangle shape and preparing it for filling in with other flowers.

8. I've filled it in with a few more daisy mums around 2 and 10 o'clock.

9. Next, I've added a few stems of alstroemeria which each have a few blooms and added three stems of Queen Anne's lace. I could add some curly willow twigs or ting ting, but I like it as it is, so I'm done!

How to Make a Large Garden Style Arrangement with Groupings

1. I'm starting with a plant tray which I painted using Colortool spray paint in a terra-cotta shade. Sometimes when you have an idea for a design and there are no containers ideally suited for it, you must use your imagination. In this case, I did not need two entire blocks of foam, so I used pieces big enough for the flowers I'm using, but not too big. This helped avoid adding excess weight to the arrangement or using more materials than necessary. As you can see I've taped my foam down in several sections.

2. I am going to establish my height with some bark material. I love the deep brown shade of the material and feel it will lend itself well to the garden style appeal. To me, it looks like the bark of an old tree. Since I have this unusual looking piece of material, it will become an "item of interest" within the arrangement.

3. I've decided to add a little more of the dark brown material. Now it looks more like a small wall. These pieces are being inserted in the back third of the foam.

4. I've done some greening with leather-leaf. I don't want to cover up too much of the foam, because I want to leave plenty of room to see where I'm putting the flowers and the moss, which will give this a garden style look.

5. I've added three large mums. You can achieve this look with many other kinds of flowers, such as roses, carnations, gerbera daisies, or any other large, single-headed flower.

6. I'm not going to stray too far from my pink and yellow hues. I've placed three large-headed carnations on the right side of the arrangement, in a similar formation but lower than the mums. I've also started to place moss into the lower front of the design.

I've used greening pins to secure the various mosses.

7. Next, as I had some gorgeous garden phlox which was exceptionally tall, I decided to make it the tallest point in my arrangement. This was one of those times when I did not choose to place my tallest flower first.

After that, to add yellow throughout the arrangement, I inserted a whole solidago flower behind the pink carnations. Yellow and mauve daisy mums have been placed lower and forward as though they are growing sideways from the arrangement.

I added more items of interest in the mossy areas with grapes and a curled, stapled hosta leaf. Long, dried poppy seed pods make a striking and stark addition to the otherwise lush arrangement. I've added more greens but kept them mostly low except for the natural living grapevine plant reaching up on the far right. To give this arrangement some extra pizzazz, I wrapped gold bullion wire around my brown columnar bark material and over and around my mosses.

I placed most of the flowers and materials in groupings to give it a natural look. Even though the flowers are evenly placed, they appear to have grown naturally there.

8. Before I cover up the mechanics in the back of the arrangement, here it is for you to see! From this point of view, you can see that most of the greens are kept lower to the ground.

All done!

Oops! Look, you can see the container peeking out under my arrangement! Tsk, tsk! Oh well, I hope it's not distracting.

It's best to cover us as much of your mechanics as possible, but don't obsess over it more than your overall arrangement. After all, this is a garden style arrangement, so it benefits from a little messiness.

Often in natural environments fresh floral material grows alongside dead or decayed wood or flowers. The poppy pods used above bloom early in the year and so sit dried and dead for most of the summer. They sit in the yard as an item of interest jutting out above an otherwise lush floral landscape.

Driftwood is used as a base and an item of interest in this wonderful arrangement. Peonies, roses, cymbidium orchids, and graceful dangling amaranthus create an unforgettable presentation piece.

Tutorials Part 3
Arrangements for Weddings & Special Occasions
How to Make a Resting Bouquet

1. We begin with about a half piece of foam already soaked and secured with floral tape. If you wanted to you could even use a piece of tape all around the outer rim. I usually do use a bit more tape to err on the side of safety and integrity.

I can't stress enough how important it is to be sure that all your flowers and mechanics are secure. You always want to make sure that your flowers are in the foam nice and firm, at least two inches deep, depending on the stem size and strength.

Inserting, removing, and then re-inserting stems or other materials is not recommended. There are a few reasons for this. One is that when you remove a stem from floral foam you create an air pocket. When that stem is re-inserted or other stems are inserted, they might not get the water they need. Another reason is that you compromise the integrity of your foam when you remove and re-insert stems too often. I would be fibbing if I said I never do it, but it should be avoided as much as possible.

2. In this example, I've taken some natural garden raspberry leaf and used its graceful curve to begin the outline of my resting bouquet. I've reinforced that line with some leather fern and a few salal stems. Balanced out to nearly the same length are a few stems I've inserted into the foam on the other side.

We will fill the middle part in eventually so that this looks as though someone has laid a sumptuous bouquet on top of a mirrored bowl. As the bowl is lavender-grey tinged, I'm going to finish off with lavender limonium filler flowers and a large lavender bow.

If possible it's good to have your container in mind before you begin your floral design work so that the colors of your design will have a better chance to blend harmoniously.

3. I'm beginning to build my structure with my first group of flowers, the always endearing gerbera daisy. I've wired some of these so that they can be bent to my will while retaining their strength and place in the arrangement. These three bright yellow gerbera daisies will be the stars of the show. They will be my main focal point in this design.

4. Building our skeletal structure, here I've inserted mini carnations to appear as though they are coming out of the bouquet and are distributed throughout.

5. Once my structural and feature/mass flowers are in place, I add in bits and pieces of solidago in and around, as though they are extending naturally from a bouquet. My final flowers are my filler flowers. In this case I've used the popular limonium, also known as caspia. It's become a recent contender to fill the role gypsophila (baby's breath) has for so long. I've extended it out slightly in a few areas to help shape the overall bouquet and give it a bit of an ethereal quality. On the other end, I've inserted enough long stems into the floral foam to represent what an actual bouquet's stems would look like.

Using the bow tying method shown here in this book, I've created a large bow with satin ribbon and attached it on the top of the floral foam with a few greening pins. Finally, I added one more length of ribbon and secured it with a greening pin to make it appear to be the ribbon's tails.

6. Here is the backstage area! It's shocking how unfinished it is, isn't it? This area will be finished off with a few well placed salal leaves and the whole thing will pull together!

7. This kind of arrangement is appropriate for occasions that call for a graceful touch, like a wedding at the guest book area or near the cake table. Other possibilities include a birthday celebration or a tea party.

How to Make a Floral Headpiece
Headpiece for Bride or Flower Girl

1. First, I've taken two medium gauge wires and twisted them together, then wrapped them with flora tape. There are different methods for creating the foundation for your headpiece. I like the idea that commonly used flower shop items, regular wire, and flora tape can empower you to create things without waiting for specially sized wires. I've sized this on my own head and I will trim the overall ends when I'm finished. You could use ribbon but it's not structurally strong, so your flowers won't have any support except for the pins you use in your hair. It's good to create something strong if possible.

2. I've chosen five green button mums, wired them through the center (as with daisies), and taped them.

3. I've chosen three alstroemeria flowers and three sprigs of yarrow, taped together with small pieces of leather fern. I've wired three small pinecones for this headpiece to give it an earthy feel. Everything has been set aside and is ready for assembly.

4. I've decided to add a small piece of grapevine wreath to the wire headpiece frame for extra effect. I've attached the grapevine to my wire frame using flora tape, but only in a few places. You don't want the grapevine to be too closely bound to the frame.

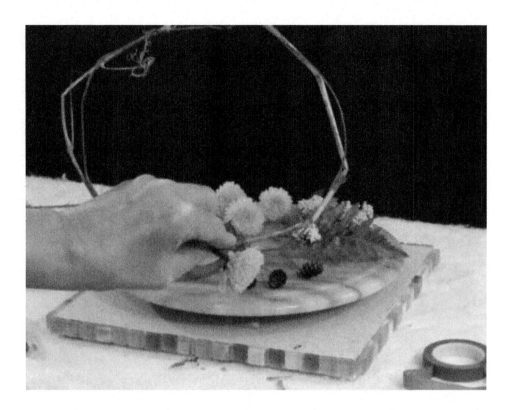

5. Now I've taped my grapevine wreath to my wire frame. I'm considering the placements of the five green button mums.

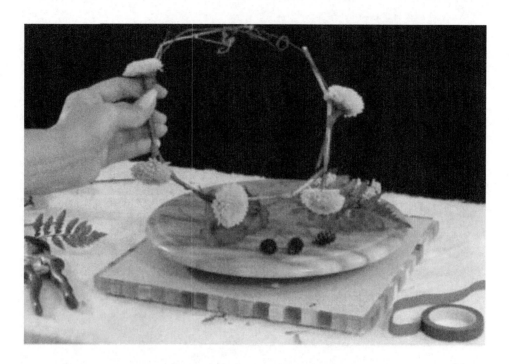

6. Here I've placed the button mums evenly. I've secured them with flora tape. This is the method I'll use for the rest of the items to be added to the headpiece.

7. I've placed all the other elements evenly and added additional bear's grass banding around the base. I thought a lavender ribbon loosely wound around and through the headpiece would make all the colors more visible. I did not tie the ribbon. As I did with all the other elements in the headpiece, I taped the ribbon on, as I did not want too much bow to take over the look.

How to Make a Small Bouquet
Easy Six Rose Bridal Bouquet

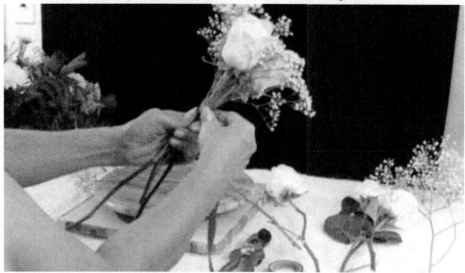

1. For this small bouquet, we begin by taping together three roses and a few sprigs of gypsophila.

2. Now I've taken three more roses and a few more sprigs of gypsophila and assembled them around the first group, adding to it and taping the whole thing together again.

3. I wanted to make a graceful-looking collar around the lower bottom of this bouquet using variegated pittosporum which would pick up the creamy white shades.

I'm trimming off a few of the gypsophila pieces which are extending out too far beyond my roses, making the bouquet look sloppy and less round.

4. After securely taping everything together one more time, I took some of my favorite thick satin ribbon and wrapped it tightly around the stems, then back up again. I inserted a few pins to finish the look and hold everything firmly in place.

By the way, be sure to point the pins upward and away from where someone's hands might accidentally touch them.

5. Our final bouquet!

6. If you are creating this bouquet for a special event, it's a good idea to provide a water source for it while it's waiting for the bride or guest of honor. Be careful not to get the ribbons wet and make sure it's not dripping when it's given to its recipient.

How to Make a Three-Piece Event Arrangement
Three-Piece Modular for Special Event

1. Here I have three identical containers which I am going to connect with a bit of unwound grapevine wreath. All our containers have been lined with plastic waterproof containers to be sure that my galvanized steel containers will not leak onto any surfaces. The water tightness of your vessel is one thing you always want to be cognizant of.

As you can see, my floral foam looks sort of messy, but since no one will see that, I can create the structural elements that I need as long as I cover up the ugly mechanics. It's the same with any structure - if you were to pull the walls and beams off of the most beautiful buildings, you would see lots of behind-the-scenes ugliness.

2. Here I have a grapevine wreath which I am going to unwind and use greening pins to secure to my floral foam. You can buy grapevine wreath from any craft store, and it's great to have around for floral uses.

3. Going along with the natural curves of the grapevine wreath, I've secured part of it to the foam and connected it to the others.

4. Now I've added my first flowers. As these flowers are huge, they are going to command attention.

5. I've added a bit of leather fern, trying not to put too much in or place it too high in the arrangement. I'm not following any pattern here, just trying to start covering my lower mechanics and add some graceful foliage.

I do want there to be a bit of negative space between the top flower heads and the foliage beneath, otherwise everything will start to look bushier than I want for this arrangement.

6. Now I've added in a Step 4 flower (gypsophila) before my Step 3 flowers. This is because if I don't, it may be harder to insert the stems of the next flowers, which are mini carnations.

I've also added a whimsical touch of natural wood-hued ting ting. I usually find that ting ting gives things a lighthearted look. As I'm going for a high-style look here, something perhaps for a gift table at a wedding, I normally would not choose ting ting, but in this case I felt it added a champagne effect. Also, the ting ting matches well with my grapevine wreath and the spirals repeat in both the grapevine and the ting ting, unifying the whole look.

This kind of arrangement is normally created on-site, but some can be assembled hours beforehand and put together at the event.

7. I've added my mini carnations in a light and airy form. I've tried to place them to extend slightly further and higher than most of my lower foliage, but I don't want them to compete too much with the commanding cremon mum heads or the negative space just below them.

Additionally, I've added a bit more leather fern to balance out the trio. Although it is good to use more than one type of foliage in some arrangements, or even most, in this case I did not use any more greens. I left the job up to the humble and elegant leather fern alone. The grapevine, ting ting, and striking placement of the cremon mums were my focus and I stopped at that point. You may find that there is a little voice inside your head that says, "that's enough," and it's done.

I want you to see this arrangement above with new eyes. Imagine other flowers and foliage you might decide to use. This kind of arrangement can be easy and relatively cost-effective to create. Imagine this idea, but perhaps with other container choices. Practice with twigs, grapevine wreath, and floral foam. If you can spend some money on a few bunches of flowers of almost any kind, some floral foam, and basic floral supplies, you can practice with the flowers you buy. When you're done, you will have an arrangement to enjoy, or even take apart and use the flowers to make more arrangements for practice! It's well worth it. Remember that it's all about learning how to handle the stems. Take time to notice the characteristics of each stem and its leaves. In floral design, choices are often made because of a stem's structural strength, rather than preferred flowers.

How to Make a Cascade Bouquet
Advanced Cascade Bridal Bouquet

1. Starting with our pre-soaked bouquet holder, we begin at the top to place our greens. After the top placement (which is kept on the low side to avoid hiding the bride's face or dress), we place the side foliage and the bottom foliage which will be longer than the other pieces as it's a cascade style bouquet.

2. Here's a side view so you can see that the foliage is inserted into the back area of the foam, right up to the edge. This picture also illustrates the gentle curve you're going for with this kind of bouquet.

3. Now I've added in four more pieces of foliage to fill in the bouquet with basic back area greening. I've used salal, but of course you can experiment with whatever foliage you like.

4. Place one rose just to the right of the top at 2 o'clock, followed by one exactly opposite at 8 o'clock, and finally place your front and center rose. This rose will extend a little higher up and become the top of the front of the arrangement.

5. I've placed roses in a zig-zag pattern down the front of the arrangement. If you find your stems are not holding in your bouquet holder, it can be good to either pin them in through the plastic on the floral foam or use florist's glue such as Floralock. Using hot glue on or near flowers is not recommended.

6. Another side view.

7. Adding in variegated pittosporum close to the base of the arrangement catches the creamy white shade of the roses and adds a lacy look.

8. Now I've moved on to my next flowers in this arrangement - flat mums. I've used my original zig-zag pattern from the roses to help me place my mums, also in a zig-zag pattern.

9. Now adding in a few stems of mini carnations, the holes are filling in nicely.

10. Finally I've dotted in some limonium (caspia).

11. But wait, there's more! I added some wired bear's grass in two spots to give a more delicate touch.

12. Here is a side view of the bear's grass additions. Notice how they extend out from the overall arrangement.

13. Here is our finished cascade bouquet. We could add ribbon if we wanted to, but sometimes no ribbon is better.

If you created this for a bride's special day, you would give it a spray of floral life extender like Crowning Glory.

Here is a wonderful example of another kind of cascade bouquet - an exotic style. Here, phalaenopsis orchids are the focal point and structural flowers. Huge green anthurium provide contrast, a base, and the look of foliage, and sweetheart roses add some elegance while doing the job of filler flower in this case.

Notice how the bride's hand is holding the handle upside down. Sometimes it is necessary to design bouquets upside down in the bouquet holder, so that they can be better handled.

Notice the accents in the bouquet above with the designed grasses and the final touch of gold wire.

CHAPTER 7: *Table Of Steps*

Step 1 All Preparation of Containers, Foams, Tapes, and Bases	Step 2 Structural and/or Line Flowers	Step 3 Feature and/or Mass Flowers	Step 4 Filler Flowers	Step 5 Greening & Finishing
Baskets	Agapanthus	Alstroemeria	Alstroemeria (individual blooms)	Adding a Bow
Pedestals	Alstroemeria stem (sometimes)	Asiatic Lily	Asters	Adding a Card
Preparing Containers	Anthurium	Asters	Daisy Mums	Bear's Grass
Stands	Asiatic Lily	Bells of Ireland	Delphinium/ Larkspur (individual stems for corsage work)	Bells of Ireland
Taping Floral Foam	Bells of Ireland	Bird of Paradise	Dendrobium Orchid (individual blooms)	Boxwood
Vases	Bird of Paradise	Daffodil	Gypsophila	Excelsior
Wire Frames	Daffodil	Daisy Mums	Hypericum	Final Wrapping
Wiring Flowers	Daisy Mums (sometimes)	Dendrobium Orchid (stem/blooms)	Large Single Carnation (sometimes)	Galax Leaf
	Delphinium (Monkshood)	Freesia	Limonium/ Caspia	Israeli Ruscus
	Delphinium (Larkspur)	Gerbera Daisy	Mini Carnations	Italian Ruscus
	Dendrobium Orchid (stem)	Ginger	Oncidium Orchid	Lace/Pearl/Gold/ Rhinestone Bullion
	Gerbera Daisy	Gladiolus (sometimes)	Queen Anne's Lace	Leather Fern

Step 1	Step 2	Step 3	Step 4	Step 5
	Ginger	Hypericum	Solidago (individual	Monstera Leaf

		blooms)	
Gladiolus	Iris	Spray Roses	Mosses/Lichens
Iris	Large Single Carnation	Statice	Palm Leaf
Large Single Carnation	Large Mums	Waxflower	Plumosa Fern
Large Mums	Liatris		Salal/ Lemon Leaf
Liatris (sometimes)	Mini Carnations (sometimes)		Ti Leaf
Oriental Lily	Oncidium Orchid		Twigs - Curly Willow
Phaelenopsis Orchid (stem)	Oriental Lily		Twigs - Dogwood
Queen Anne's Lace (on stem, sometimes)	Phaelenopsis Orchid (individual blooms)		Variegated Pittosporum
Roses	Queen Anne's Lace		
Snapdragon	Ranunculus		
Solidago (entire stem, sometimes)	Roses		
Stock	Snapdragon		
Tuberose	Solidago		
Tulip	Spray Roses		
	Statice		
	Stock		
	Tuberose		
	Tulip		

Printed in Great Britain
by Amazon

36353495R00117